T0282283

VISUAL EXPLORER GUIDE

ANCIENT
ROME

VISUAL EXPLORER GUIDE

ANCIENT
ROME

CLAUDIA MARTIN

amber
BOOKS

First published in 2023

Published by
Amber Books Ltd
United House
North Road
London
N7 9DP
United Kingdom
www.amberbooks.co.uk
Instagram: amberbooksltd
Facebook: amberbooks
Twitter: @amberbooks
Pinterest: amberbooksltd

Project Editor: Michael Spilling
Designer: Keren Harragan
Picture Research: Terry Forshaw

ISBN: 978-1-83886-300-5

Printed in China

Contents

Introduction

Founded in the 8th century BCE, ancient Rome grew from a small Italic settlement on the Tiber River to a vast metropolis home to as many as a million people. Over the centuries, the city took control over its neighbours through a mixture of military, commercial, cultural and political might. At its peak, Rome's empire had 50 to 90 million inhabitants, one-fifth of the world's population. Until 509 BCE, Rome was ruled by kings who are said to have been elected by the populace – until the last of them, Lucius Tarquinius Superbus, took the throne by force, leading to the establishment of the Republic. Rome's Republic centred on annually elected magistrates, the most important being two consuls, who worked with the Senate, initially a council of the nobility, known as patricians. After this delicate balance was ripped apart by civil war, the first emperor, Augustus, took control in 27 BCE. A long line of emperors followed until, in 476 CE, the barbarian king Odoacer deposed the last emperor of the Western Roman Empire, Romulus Augustulus.

ABOVE:
Ramp of Domitian
Domitian's 1st-century CE ramp linked the Forum with the Palatine Hill.

OPPOSITE:
Appian Way
This 560-km (350-mile) road was begun by censor Appius Claudius Caecus in 312 BCE.

The Forum

Often referred to today as the Forum Romanum, this great plaza was known to the citizens of ancient Rome as the Forum Magnum, or simply the Forum. The rectangular square, surrounded by magnificent government and religious buildings, was the heart of ancient Rome. It was the venue for politics, business, trials, speeches and processions. This area was the focus of Roman life from the days of the Roman Kingdom (c.753–509 BCE), when it was home to the royal palace, known as the Regia, and the Temple of Vesta, both of which were rebuilt in Imperial times. From the 7th century BCE until after the Fall of Rome in 476 CE, the Senate met in a Curia building on the Forum. Republican times saw the construction of the first basilicas around the Forum, from roughly 184 BCE. These immense public buildings were used for legal proceedings, as well as business. The Forum took its final form with the prodigious building and reconstruction carried out by the first emperor, Augustus (27 BCE–14 CE). Imperial times also saw some commercial and legal business move away from the overcrowded Forum Magnum to other fora, today known collectively as the Imperial Fora. After 476 CE, the Forum Magnum was slowly abandoned and – along with much of Rome – began to fall into ruin. As the ground level rose, many of the Forum's structures were dismantled and recycled. Excavation began in the 19th century.

OPPOSITE:
The Forum
The shape and form of the Forum changed over the centuries. By Imperial times, the towering public buildings had reduced the central plaza to a rectangle around 130 by 50m (425 by 165ft).

Tarpeian Rock
This cliff, on the south side of the Capitoline Hill and looming above the Forum, was used for hurling traitors and murderers to their deaths until the 1st century CE. The phrase *Arx Tarpeia Capitoli proxima* ('The Tarpeian Rock is close to the Capitol') was a reminder that ignominy can follow swiftly on success.

Temple of Saturn and Temple of Vespasian and Titus

The Temple of Saturn (far left) is at the western end of the Forum. Although a temple to the god stood on the site from 497 BCE, the current ruins date from 360 CE. The Temple of Vespasian and Titus (right) was squeezed into a narrow gap next door, honouring the deified emperors Vespasian (69–79 CE) and his son Titus (79–81 CE).

ABOVE AND OPPOSITE:

Arch of Septimius Severus

Around 23m (75ft) high, this triumphal arch, at the
north-western end of the Forum, commemorated the
victories of Emperor Septimius Severus and his sons
against the Parthians, in 194–195 CE and 197–199 CE.
Winged victories adorn the spandrels.

OPPOSITE:
Column of Phocas
The last addition to the Forum was the 13.6-m (44-ft) Corinthian column honouring the Byzantine Emperor Phocas in 608 CE. The column, carved in the 2nd century CE for an unknown building, was once topped by a gilded statue of the emperor.

LEFT:
Curia Julia
Built between 44 and 29 CE by Julius Caesar and his successor Augustus, the Senate house is one of the few ancient Roman structures to survive largely intact. This is in no small part due to the Curia's conversion into the church of Sant'Adriano al Foro in the 7th century.

Basilica Julia

This 100-m (328-ft) long public building was constructed along the south side of the Forum from 46 BCE, but most of the ruins date from the 3rd century CE. The basilica housed law courts, offices, meeting rooms and shops. Little but the foundations remain of the once three-storey building. Three columns of the Temple of Castor and Pollux can be seen in the background.

ABOVE:
Decennalia, Five-Columns Monument
Dedicated in 303 CE, the surviving portion of this monument depicts an animal sacrifice.

RIGHT:
Rostra
This platform was where politicians, magistrates and other orators delivered their addresses to the people of Rome.

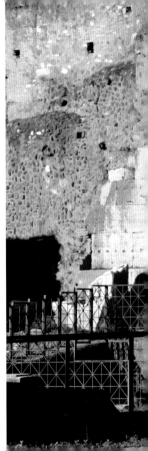

Basilica Aemilia

Named after consul Marcus Aemilius Lepidus, the basilica contained shops and a main hall 100m (328ft) long and 30m (98ft) wide. It was rebuilt many times between 200 BCE and 420 CE.

Western Forum
The domed Santi Luca e Martina (centre left) was dedicated to St Martina in the 7th century. Martina was martyred in 228 CE under the Severan dynasty, who built the adjacent triumphal arch.

ABOVE:
Temple of Caesar
Flowers are often placed on the remains of the altar
of the deified Julius Caesar. At the eastern end of the
Forum square, the temple was dedicated by Caesar's
successor, Augustus, in 29 BCE.

OPPOSITE:
Temple of Vesta
This circular temple housed the sacred flame of the
goddess Vesta, virgin goddess of the hearth, home and
family. It was rebuilt many times between possibly the
7th century BCE and the late 2nd century CE.

Temple of Castor and Pollux

The remaining Corinthian columns of the Temple of Castor and Pollux tower over the ruins of Basilica Julia. Much of the temple dates from the time of Tiberius (14–37 CE), who rebuilt it after a fire destroyed an earlier structure. In Greek and Roman mythology, Castor and Pollux were twin sons of Spartan queen Leda.

RIGHT:
**House of the
Vestal Virgins**
Behind the Temple of
Vesta, this palace housed
the women who tended
Vesta's flame. If one of the
Vestals broke her vow of
chastity, she was punished
by being buried alive.

OVERLEAF LEFT:
Umbilicus Urbis
Once encased in marble,
this 3rd-century CE
structure marked the
symbolic centre of Rome,
from which all distances
were measured.

OVERLEAF RIGHT:
Milliarium Aureum
Built in 20 BCE, the
'Golden Milestone'
served a similar purpose
to the Umbilicus Urbis,
symbolizing the starting
point of the road system.

ALL PHOTOGRAPHS:
Tabularium
On the slope of the
Capitoline Hill, the 8th-
century BCE Tabularium
(records office) forms
the foundation of the
Capitoline Museums'
medieval Palazzo
Senatorio (centre back).

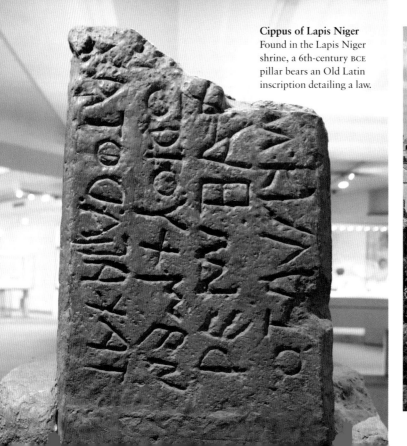

Cippus of Lapis Niger
Found in the Lapis Niger shrine, a 6th-century BCE pillar bears an Old Latin inscription detailing a law.

PREVIOUS PAGE AND RIGHT:
Basilica of Maxentius
The largest of the Forum basilicas, this secular building was begun by Maxentius and completed by Constantine I in 312 CE. Like other Roman basilicas, it featured a huge meeting space in the central nave. Although most had a roof supported by columns, it was built using arches, a style more commonly seen in public baths of the period.

Palatine Hill

The central hill among Rome's seven hills, the Palatine rises on the south side of the Forum. The hill was inhabited from at least the 10th century BCE and may well have been the core of the settlement that became Rome. During the Republican period (c. 509–27 BCE), when the city's business hub lay in the nearby Forum, many wealthy Romans built their homes in the clean air of the Palatine. From the start of the Imperial period, the hill was the location of the emperors' palaces. In fact, the Palatine came to be so associated with palaces that it gave us the word 'palace'. The first imperial palace here was that of the first emperor, Augustus. This was followed by the palace of his successor, Tiberius (14–37 CE), which was partly incorporated into the palace of Nero (54–68 CE) known as the Domus Transitoria, which was partly overbuilt by the palace of Domitian (81–96 CE). This vast palace – extended and remodelled – remained the imperial residence until the 5th century. The palace was in three main parts: the public wing, known today as the Domus Flavia; the private wing, the Domus Augustana; and the garden, often called the 'stadium'. The final extension, commissioned by Septimius Severus (193–211 CE), entailed the construction of an immense platform as there was no more room on the hill. After the Fall of Rome in 476 BCE, the palaces were abandoned and partly built over by villas, gardens and a convent.

OPPOSITE:
North-west Palatine Hill
The ancient retaining walls of the hill rise over the Forum. This side of the hill was home to the Domus Tiberiana, but its remnants were largely buried under a viewing platform built in 1550 by Cardinal Farnese.

Via Nova

Along with Via Sacra, which stretched from the Colosseum to the Capitoline Hill, Via Nova was one of the Forum's main streets. 'New Road' runs beneath the Palatine Hill, which was reached by a ramp and steps.

OPPOSITE AND OVERLEAF:
Palace of Domitian

This palace was built as Domitian's residence in 81–92 CE. With additions, it was the imperial residence until the 5th century. Pictured opposite are the foundations of the banquet hall, or *cenatio*, in the Domus Flavia wing; and overleaf a peristyle garden with a pool featuring an Amazonian shield design, in the Domus Augustana portion of the palace.

LEFT, ABOVE AND OVERLEAF:
Palace of Septimius Severus
The final extension to the Palatine Hill's imperial palace
was by Septimius Severus (193–211 CE). Substantial brick
structures at the southern corner of the hill remain. The
complex's rooms, terraces and gardens offered views
over the Circus Maximus below.

Palace of Septimius Severus
Severus gained power after a period
of civil war. He strengthened his claim
with building projects including his
grandiose palace, which was originally
encased in marble and overlooked the
crowds in the Circus Maximus.

Garden of Domitian

Often known as the Stadium of Domitian (not to be confused with the Stadium of Domitian near the Campus Martius), this garden was the last part of the imperial palace built by Domitian. It looks like a Roman circus but was too small for chariots, although it may have been used for horseriding.

A portico ran around the perimeter of the garden, which was adorned with numerous statues.

LEFT:

Domus Tiberiana

The most visible remains of the palace of Tiberius are arcaded support structures on the side of the hill. At the bottom of the slope is a vestibule, built by Domitian and Hadrian, from where a ramp led up to the palace.

OVERLEAF:

Domus Transitoria

This was the first palace of Nero (54–68 CE), damaged by the Great Fire of 64. Surviving chambers include the latrines (overleaf top right).

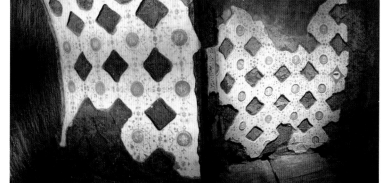

BOTH PHOTOGRAPHS:
Domus Aurea
From around 60 CE, decadent Emperor Nero built a palace extending from the Palatine to the Esquiline hills, at first called Domus Transitoria. That palace was burned down soon after completion, then rebuilt, vastly extended and renamed the 'Golden House' for its huge golden dome. The remains of the 300-room, 50-hectare (123-acre) estate can be visited north of the Colosseum.

Leisure

To enhance their reputation and to keep the populace happy, emperors and other leading Romans sponsored public entertainments, as well as the immense venues required to stage them. The Colosseum was the largest venue for gladiatorial contests and other, often violent, games. The Circus Maximus was the key venue for chariot- and horse-racing, as well as wild animal shows and festivals. Chariot-racing was the most popular Roman sport, with the spectators fanatically cheering and cursing their favourite team, idolizing the charioteers and placing bets, much in the manner of modern football supporters. Some higher-brow entertainments took place in theatres, where there were performances of comedies, tragedies and music. For wealthier Romans, other ways to spend leisure time were fishing, handball, hunting, board games and gambling, as well as music, dancing and poetry performances at dinner parties. For the less wealthy, taverns offered drink, food and a game of dice. For men both rich and poor, there were also countless licensed brothels. Public bathhouses were central to the lives of men of all classes, as well as many women. Even if the wealthy owned their own bath, they still used the public amenities, often taking a slave to protect their belongings. Public bathhouses were not only for bathing but for socializing, exercising, reading in the library and sharing food in the restaurant.

OPPOSITE:
The Colosseum
The largest amphitheatre ever built, the Colosseum was constructed and modified by the three emperors of the Flavian dynasty (69–96 CE): Vespasian, Titus and Domitian. It could hold 50,000 to 80,000 spectators.

RIGHT AND OVERLEAF:
The Colosseum
This amphitheatre
was used for public
entertainments including
gladiatorial contests,
executions, animal hunts
and re-enactments of
famous battles. The
oval arena itself had a
wooden floor covered by
sand (arena means 'sand'
in Latin). Beneath the
floor was the hypogeum
('underground'), a two-
storey labyrinth of tunnels
and cages for holding
gladiators and animals,
with shafts, pulleys and
elevators for access to
ground level.

Ludus Magnus

Close to the Colosseum and linked to it by a tunnel, this was the largest of Rome's gladiatorial schools. It was built by Domitian (81–96 CE) and remodelled by later emperors. Gladiators from across the empire lived here while they practised their skills in the ellipsoidal arena.

BOTH PHOTOGRAPHS:
Amphitheatrum Castrense
Built in the early 3rd century CE, this amphitheatre was part of a villa complex used by emperors of the Severan dynasty (193–235 CE). In the late 3rd century, the open arches of the walls were bricked up when the building stopped being used for spectacles and was incorporated into the Aurelian city walls.

Circus Maximus
Holding 150,000 spectators, this chariot-racing stadium was 621m (2037ft) long. Games were held in this valley from the days of the Roman Kingdom. Stone seating was added from the early 2nd century BCE.

LEFT:

Circus Maximus

Only a small segment remains of the stadium, which was rebuilt more than once after the Great Fire of Rome in 64 CE, which began in nearby shops. Visible today are parts of a seating tier, curved turn and central barrier.

RIGHT:

Roman Houses of the Caelian Hill

These rooms, now underground, were originally part of an apartment block, known as an *insula*, but were converted into a luxurious and vibrantly frescoed patrician home in the 3rd century CE. The site gives a unique insight into the life of Rome's upper class.

RIGHT:

Circus of Maxentius

At 503m (1650ft) long, this was the second largest racing venue, after the Circus Maximus. Emperor Maxentius built the circus just past the second mile of the Appian Way, in 306–312 CE. The only known games staged here honoured the death of Maxentius's teenage son Valerius Romulus, who died in 309.

OPPOSITE:

Baths of Diocletian

Built in 298–306 CE, during the reign of co-emperors Diocletian and Maximian, these were the largest public baths in Rome. Supplied with water by the Aqua Marcia aqueduct, the baths contained a *frigidarium*, *tepidarium*, *caldarium*, gymnasium and libraries.

Baths of Caracalla
Built between 212 and 216/7 CE, these public baths were used until the 530s. The complex measured 337 by 328m (1106 by 1076ft). As well as areas for bathing, swimming, wrestling and relaxing, there were libraries and shops.

Baths of Trajan

The baths commissioned by Emperor Trajan (98–117 CE) were built over a portion of the ruins of Nero's extravagant and hated Domus Aurea palace. The main bath chambers were in a sequence along a south-west to north-east axis: *caldarium* (cold room), *tepidarium* (warm room), *frigidarium* (hot room) and *natatio* (swimming pool).

BOTH PHOTOGRAPHS:
Theatre of Marcellus
Used for performances of music and drama, this theatre was named after the late nephew of Emperor Augustus, who formally inaugurated the building in 12 BCE. The theatre, which could hold an audience of around 17,500, was built from brick, concrete and tuff, then faced in travertine.

82

OPPOSITE:

Porticus Octaviae

Close to the Theatre of Marcellus, Emperor Augustus built this portico in the name of his sister Octavia, mother of Marcellus. The portico enclosed two pre-existing temples, as well as a library, numerous works of art, and lecture and meeting rooms.

RIGHT:

Hadrian's Villa

Emperor Hadrian (117–138 CE) disliked the imperial palace on the Palatine Hill, so commissioned a vast country retreat 29km (18 miles) away, at modern-day Tivoli. From c.128 CE, he governed from the estate, which boasted more than 30 buildings, countless statues, gardens, fountains and baths.

Hadrian's Villa

Hadrian was a well-travelled emperor who commissioned buildings and art inspired by places that held personal significance. The Canopus (opposite) was named after the Egyptian city where his lover Antinous drowned. Its reflecting pool, representing the Nile, was surrounded by copies of famous sculptures from across the empire. The 'Golden Hall' held a dining room (right) and library, topped with concrete domes that were possibly designed by the emperor himself.

LEFT AND OVERLEAF:
Villa of the Quintilii
In the mid-2nd century CE, the wealthy Quintilius brothers built an immense country estate between the fifth and sixth milestones of the Appian Way. The villa's baths (overleaf left) were fed by their own aqueduct. The *nymphaeum* (left) served as a formal assembly room. Emperor Commodus so admired the villa that he had the owners executed and confiscated it for himself.

BOTH PHOTOGRAPHS:
Villa of Livia
A country retreat owned by Emperor Augustus's wife Livia Drusilla (59 BCE–29 CE), the Villa of Livia is north of central Rome, at Prima Porta. Lovely frescoes of a verdant garden with pomegranate trees and ornamental plants have been removed to the Palazzo Massimo alle Terme of the Museo Nazionale Romano.

BOTH PHOTOGRAPHS:

Capo di Bove

Excavations at Capo di Bove, on the outskirts of modern
Rome, have revealed the remains of thermal baths built
in the 2nd century CE as part of an estate owned by
consul Herodes Atticus and his wife Annia Regilla.

BOTH PHOTOGRAPHS:

Baths of Nero

First built in 62 or 64 CE, the popular Baths of Nero lay on the Campus Martius. Little remains of the structure today, but fragments have been scattered across the quarter. Two granite columns stand in the Via di Sant'Eustachio (left) while the Fontana del Senato (right), on Via degli Staderari, has reused a basin that probably stood in the *caldarium*.

Monuments and Statues

Perhaps more than any cultural group before or since, the ancient Romans sought to immortalize themselves by making their mark on this earth, as if saying to everyone who came later: 'I was here.' This desire can be seen in the ancient city's toweringly hubristic and costly triumphal arches, columns and mausoleums. Yet the same drive appears to have been felt by all classes and manifested itself in ways that the elite must have seen as tasteless, from the graffiti of countless jokers to the bakery-inspired tomb of a freed slave and the Nubian-style pyramid of a magistrate. Roman sculpture was significantly influenced by Greek sculpture, as can be seen by the number of artworks that are copies of,

or heavily inspired by, Greek originals. Yet while Greek sculpture sought to idealize the human form, the purpose of many Roman sculptures was to immortalize – whether by advertising the subject's power or heroism, as in the *Colossus of Constantine* or the ridiculous *Commodus as Hercules*; or by showing off their sponsor's wealth and taste, as evidenced by the hundreds of public statues that turned Rome into a vast gallery. In the early days of Rome, most sculptures were in terracotta or bronze, but from the 2nd century BCE, many were in Paros or Carrara marble. Originally, most were painted in bright colours. While the statues' paint has faded, the evidence of their artists' and patrons' ambition has not.

OPPOSITE:
Trajan's Column
This column celebrates the victory of Trajan in the Dacian Wars (101–102, 105–106 CE), which are depicted in the 190-m (620-ft) long spiralling bas relief. The Dacians lived in the region of Romania and Moldova.

LEFT:

Trajan's Column

Trajan's Column was erected in 113 CE in the newly completed Trajan's Forum, both the work of Nabataean architect Apollodorus of Damascus. The column was originally topped by a statue of Trajan, which disappeared in the Middle Ages. Since 1587, it has been capped by a statue of St Peter the Apostle.

RIGHT:

Castel Sant'Angelo

This museum and erstwhile papal fortress was originally the mausoleum of Emperor Hadrian. Constructed between 134 and 139 CE, the cylindrical building was the repository for urns holding the ashes of Hadrian, his wife and son, and several successors.

RIGHT:
**Column of
Marcus Aurelius**
Modelled on Trajan's
column, the victory
column of Marcus
Aurelius (161–180 CE)
bears a spiralling relief
depicting the Danubian or
Marcomannic Wars. The
column was constructed
from immense blocks of
Carrara marble, hollowed
out for a stairway to the
platform at the top.

FAR RIGHT:
**Mausoleum
of Maxentius**
Built by Emperor
Maxentius (306–312 CE),
this rotunda was the
burial place of the
emperor's teenage son,
Valerius Romulus. The
lack of interior decoration
suggests the mausoleum
was never completed.

Mausoleum of Augustus
Built in 28 BCE, this circular mausoleum was one of Augustus's first building projects in Rome after his victory over Mark Antony and Cleopatra at the Battle of Actium in 31 BCE. Augustus was the first Roman emperor, initiator of the imperial cult as well as an era of broadly imperial peace, the Pax Augusta.

Mausoleum of Augustus

This mausoleum was constructed from concentric rings of soil and brick, then faced with travertine. It may originally have had a conical roof topped by a bronze statue of Augustus. An inner chamber held golden urns containing the ashes of Augustus and his close family, as well as his successors Tiberius, Caligula, Claudius and Nerva.

RIGHT:
Mausoleum of Helena
This mausoleum was
the resting place of
Constantine I's mother
Helena, who died in
330 CE. Helena, who made
a pilgrimage to the Holy
Land, is considered a saint
by the Catholic Church.

OPPOSITE:
Arch of Janus
This early 4th-century CE
quadrifons (with a gate on
four sides) arch may have
been a triumphal arch or a
shelter for Forum Boarium
cattle traders.

OVERLEAF LEFT:
Column of Antoninus
Only the base remains
of the column dedicated
to Antoninus Pius
(138–161 CE). It depicts
the emperor and his wife
being carried to the gods
by a winged genius.

Pyramid of Cestius
In around 18–12 BCE, priest and magistrate Gaius Cestius constructed a pyramid as his tomb. Cestius had possibly served in Nubia in 23 BCE, where he was inspired by the pyramids of Meroë.

LEFT AND ABOVE:
Arch of Titus
This 81 CE triumphal arch celebrated the victory of Emperor Titus and his father Vespasian in the First Jewish–Roman War.

OVERLEAF LEFT:
Arch of Constantine
The largest Roman triumphal arch, 21m (69ft) high, this marked Constantine I's victory over Maxentius in 312 CE.

OVERLEAF RIGHT:
Arch of Drusus
Long misidentified and misnamed, this is probably all that remains of the once-triple Arch of Trajan (98–117 CE).

LEFT:
Tomb of Eurysaces
In around 50–20 BCE, the former slave Eurysaces the Baker built a tomb that may well have been considered idiosyncratic by the Roman elite. Nothing is known about Eurysaces except his trade, but he must have become a wealthy man. The circular openings in the upper storey may represent kneading basins or grain-measuring bowls.

RIGHT:
Colossus of Constantine
The giant statue of Constantine I enthroned was constructed in 312–315 CE for the Basilica of Maxentius. Portions of the head, arms and legs – which were carved from white marble – survive, while the brick-and-wood body has not.

BOTH PHOTOGRAPHS:
Colossus of Constantine
Since the marble head of Constantine is 2.5m (8.2ft) tall, the full height of the intact statue must have been around 12m (39ft). The emperor was depicted with immense eyes that symbolize his godlike, all-seeing status, but the chin, nose and jaw are similar to more naturalistic depictions of Constantine.

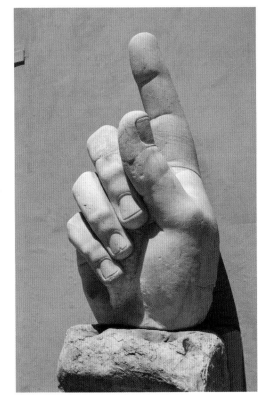

RIGHT:
**Equestrian Statue
of Marcus Aurelius**
Cast in 174–175 CE,
this bronze statue is
preserved in the Capitoline
Museums, while a replica
stands in the Piazza del
Campidoglio. Emperor
and Stoic philosopher
Marcus Aurelius
(161–180 CE) raises his
hand in *adlocutio* (salute)
to his troops. Most bronze
Roman statues were
melted down in medieval
times, but this survived as
it was misidentified as the
Christian Constantine I.

OPPOSITE LEFT AND RIGHT:
Flaminio Obelisk
Pharaoh Seti I (c.1290–
1279 BCE) and his son
Ramesses II commissioned
this obelisk, which was
brought to Rome on
the orders of Emperor
Augustus in 10 BCE.

119

Tomb of Caecilia Metella

The mausoleum was built in 30–10 BCE by consul Marcus Licinius Crassus for his mother. Standing on a hill at the three-mile marker of the Appian Way, the mausoleum is a cylindrical drum on a square podium, with the 14th-century Caetani Castle joined at the rear. The diameter of the drum is 100 Roman feet, equal to 29.5m (97ft).

Lateran Obelisk
Completed by Pharaoh Thutmose IV (1400–1390 BCE), the obelisk was erected at the Circus Maximus by Constantius II in 357 CE. After crumbling and falling, it was re-erected near the Lateran Palace in 1588.

Pupienus Maximus
Pupienus was co-emperor in 238 CE, the Year of the Six Emperors. His 99-day reign ended when he was hacked to death by the Praetorian Guard.

Commodus as Hercules
This bust of handsome, narcissistic Emperor Commodus was carved in 192 CE. Commodus sought to associate himself with the divine hero's prowess.

Marforio

This 1st-century CE marble sculpture probably depicts a river god. It may take its modern name from the Marfuoli family, who owned the land where it was originally sited, near the Forum. In the 16th century, Marforio became one of Rome's 'talking statues' with the start of the ongoing tradition of affixing satirical poems and statements to the city's famous statues.

RIGHT:

Capitoline Wolf
Housed in the Capitoline
Museums, the famous
sculpture depicts the
mythical twin founders
of Rome, Romulus and
Remus, with the she-wolf
who rescued them after
they were abandoned to
die by their great-uncle,
King Amulius. The bronze
twins were added in the
late 15th century, whereas
the she-wolf herself may
be an Etruscan work.

FAR RIGHT:

Boy with Thorn
This bronze sculpture was
probably cast by a Roman
artist in the 1st century CE,
inspired by earlier Greek
carvings of the same
subject. It is likely the
statue was intended purely
as a beautiful study of the
human body engaged in a
complex action.

Religion

The earliest forms of the Roman religion were animistic, based in an array of gods and spirits that inhabited all people and things. As contact with the Greeks grew during the Republican period, Roman gods were associated with Greek gods and took on their attributes. Then, as the empire expanded, the Romans often adopted additional gods from their new subjects. Deceased emperors were also frequently deified by their successors, creating an increasingly dominant imperial cult. Ancient Roman religion focused on prayer and sacrifices conducted at temples and household shrines, largely to gain divine favour. The priesthood and state were tightly interwoven. State policy towards Christianity, after its arrival in the 1st century CE, was largely negative, with persecution peaking under Diocletian (284–305). Changing Roman beliefs can be traced through burial customs. For most of Republican and early Imperial times, a body was cremated after death, with the remains kept in an urn and placed in a tomb or pit outside the city due to a ban on burials within Rome. From the 2nd century CE, wealthy pagans and Christians – who wanted to preserve the body for resurrection – placed their loved-ones in sarcophagi. Christians of all classes were buried in underground cemeteries known as catacombs. After Christianity became the state religion in 380, catacombs and sarcophagi declined as the dead were commonly buried in church cemeteries.

OPPOSITE:
The Pantheon
Constructed by Hadrian in around 126 CE, the Pantheon (temple 'of all the gods') was converted into a church in 609 CE. The coffered dome, with its central oculus, is still the world's largest unreinforced concrete dome.

The Pantheon

The interior of the Pantheon is lit only by the oculus and doorway, a choice perhaps intended to direct worshippers' thoughts towards the heavens and the passing of time, marked by the shifting light. The floor is tilted by 30cm (12in) so that rain falling through the oculus runs into drains. The height to the oculus and the diameter of the interior circle are both 43m (141ft).

The Pantheon

The inscription on the Pantheon's portico reads: 'M[arcus] Agrippa L[ucii] f[ilius] co[n]s[ul] tertium fecit'. This means: 'Marcus Agrippa, son of Lucius, made this when consul for the third time.' Yet it is believed that Hadrian chose to reuse this inscription from an earlier, Agrippan temple that burned down.

BOTH PHOTOGRAPHS:

Temple of Romulus

Following a fire in 306 CE, Emperor Maxentius undertook a major building programme. He dedicated this new circular temple to his deified son, Valerius Romulus, who died in 309. The temple was re-dedicated to the Christian martyrs Cosmas and Damian in 527.

Temple of Hercules Victor

Dedicated in around 143–132 BCE, this circular temple to 'Hercules the Winner' was possibly commissioned by general and consul Lucius Mummius. It is a *tholos*: a Greek-style round structure surrounded by a ring of columns supporting a domed or conical roof.

Temple of Hercules Victor

Nineteen of the original twenty Corinthian columns of this temple are largely intact. The Corinthian order is characterized by slender fluted columns with elaborate capitals decorated with scrolls and acanthus leaves. Much of the original cella (inner chamber of the temple) wall remains, but the tiled roof is a modern addition.

BOTH PHOTOGRAPHS:

Temple of Antoninus and Faustina

The temple dedicated to the deified Emperor Antoninus Pius and his wife, Faustina the Elder, was constructed from 141 CE. The building became a church possibly in the 7th century. Today, the Corinthian columns of the temple portico jut from the facade of the Chiesa di San Lorenzo in Miranda, which occupies the original cella.

Temple of Hadrian
Built in the Campus Martius ('Field of Mars') quarter of ancient Rome, this temple was dedicated to the deified Emperor Hadrian by successor Antoninus Pius in 145 CE. One wall of the cella and eleven Corinthian columns survive. The cella wall became part of a 19th-century palazzo.

BOTH PHOTOGRAPHS:

Temple of Venus and Roma

Constructed in 121–141 CE between the Forum and Colosseum, the temple to goddesses Venus and Roma Aeterna ('Eternal Rome') was probably Rome's largest, measuring 110m by 53m (360 by 174ft). It had two cellae (inner chambers), one for each goddess. In each cella was a statue of its goddess enthroned, the two statues back to back with the cellae forming mirror images of each other. Venus represented love, or *amor* in Latin, which is Roma spelled backwards, creating an additional mirror imaging.

Esquiline Venus
Emperor Claudius
(41–54 CE) may have
commissioned this
sculpture for the
Lamian Gardens on
the Esquiline Hill. The
statue is probably a
copy of a 1st-century
BCE work, possibly from
the Ptolemaic Kingdom
of Egypt, a hypothesis
supported by the Egyptian
cobra on the vase.

Temple of Portunus
The temple to Portunus,
god of livestock, was by
the Forum Boarium cattle
market and overlooking
the Tiber, so the god
could watch arriving cattle
barges. Erected in 120–80
BCE, the temple's columns
are in the Ionic style, with
scroll-like ornaments
known as volutes.

Bocca della Verità
'The Mouth of Truth' leans against the wall of Santa Maria in Cosmedin, on the site of the ancient Forum Boarium cattle market. The marble mask probably depicts the face of the river and sea god Oceanus. It may once have served as a drain cover in the nearby Temple of Hercules Victor or Forum Boarium. In medieval times, the story grew that any liar who placed their hand in the mask's mouth would have it bitten off.

**Temple of
Apollo Sosianus**
Three columns have
been re-erected from the
Campus Martius's Temple
of Apollo. Although
earlier temples to Apollo
stood on the site, these
columns probably
date from the redesign
commissioned in around
34 BCE by the wealthy
general and politician
Gaius Sosius.

LEFT AND OVERLEAF:
Largo di Torre Argentina
This square holds the
remains of four temples
and the Theatre of
Pompey, all dated to the
Republican era. Temple
A (left) is probably the
Temple of Juturna,
goddess of wells, built by
Gaius Lutatius Catulus
after his victory against
Carthage in 241 BCE.

Ara Pacis Augustae

The Altar of Augustan Peace was commissioned in 13 BCE to honour the return of Emperor Augustus to Rome after three years on campaign. Within walls sculpted in Carrara marble, the open-air altar was the site of animal sacrifices. Small openings (left) at the base of the walls on either side of the entrances were drains allowing blood to be washed away. The so-called Tellus Panel (above) probably depicts Pax, goddess of peace. Augustus popularized the worship of Pax to signal that the previous years of civil war were over.

Santa Costanza
This 4th-century church
was probably built
during the reign of the
first Christian emperor,
Constantine I. Tradition
has it the church was
originally a mausoleum
for Contantine's daughter
Constantina, who died
in 354. She was later
venerated as a saint due
to a medieval legend that
she was cured of leprosy
after praying at the tomb
of St Agnes, which lay in
catacombs beneath the
church. Built of brick-
faced concrete, Santa
Costanza has a circular
ambulatory around a
central drum topped by
a shallow dome.

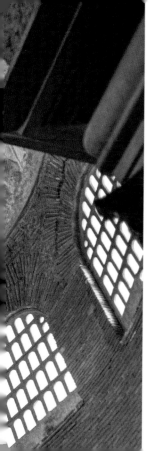

Santa Pudenziana

The oldest place of Christian worship in Rome, Santa Pudenziana is entered below modern street level (overleaf left). Probably built when Pius I (140–155 CE) was Bishop of Rome, the structure lies over an earlier house and reused part of a public bath dating to the reign of Hadrian (117–138 CE). The belltower and dome were added in the 13th and 14th centuries. The extraordinary mosaic in the apse (right) dates from around the end of the 4th century and depicts Christ as a classical Roman teacher.

DOMINVS ECCLESIAE
CONSER PVDENTI
VATOR ANAE

L

163

Catacombs of Priscilla
Pope Francis visits the
Catacombs of Priscilla,
which were used for
Christian burials from the
late 2nd century through
the 4th century. Said to be
named after the wife of
a late 1st-century consul
who was an early convert
and martyr, the catacombs
were the burial place for
early popes including
Marcellinus (296–304).

LEFT:
Catacombs of Domitilla
These catacombs were
named after 1st-century
noblewoman Flavia
Domitilla, revered for
denying the Roman gods.
Paintings in the 'Room of
the Bakers' depict the life
of a baker, showcasing the
importance of bread in
both Christian and
pagan symbolism.

BOTH PHOTOGRAPHS:
Catacombs of Via Latina
Rediscovered in 1955, these small catacombs along the ancient Via Latina date from the 4th century. The catacombs may have been owned by a single family or fraternity. Paintings include both pagan stories, depicting the hero Hercules, and scenes from the Old and New Testaments, including the Crossing of the Red Sea (opposite).

BOTH PHOTOGRAPHS:
Catacombs of Callixtus
Probably organized by Pope Callixtus (218–222 CE), these catacombs contain the Crypt of the Popes (left), where nine 3rd-century popes were interred. Nearby is the Crypt of St Cecelia, where 9th-century frescoes depict Christ and St Urban (right), who followed Callixtus as pope.

BOTH PHOTOGRAPHS:

Catacombs of Marcellinus and Peter

Situated along the ancient Via Labicana, these 4th-century catacombs contain 4.5km (2.8 miles) of underground galleries on three levels. They are said to have been the burial place of saints Marcellinus and Peter, who were executed during the Diocletianic Persecution (303–13). Paintings include Jesus Healing the Bleeding Woman (left) and the Good Shepherd (opposite). In the latter, Christ is surrounded by vignettes of the story of Jonah and figures in the orant pose, the standard attitude of prayer adopted by early Christians.

ALL PHOTOGRAPHS:
**Catacombs of
San Sebastiano**
Beneath the basilica of
San Sebastiano Fuori le
Mura, the eponymous
catacombs were used for
pagan burials from the
2nd century. In the area
known as the Piazzola
('Little Square'), which
was then an abandoned
opencast mine, are the
mausoleums of three
wealthy freedmen (far
left). The Piazzola was
later filled in and the mine
used for Christian burials.

BOTH PHOTOGRAPHS:

Casal Rotondo

Dated to around 30 BCE, Casal Rotondo is a circular mausoleum that may have been the resting place for the ashes of general Marcus Valerius Messalla Corvinus (64 BCE–8/12 CE), although most archaeologists now believe otherwise. Near the mausoleum, 19th-century archaeologist Luigi Canina built a brick wall (right) containing fragments he believed to be from Casal Rotondo, but were possibly from nearby monuments.

LEFT:
Esquiline Necropolis
The necropolis on the Esquiline Hill was in use from the 8th century BCE to the 1st century CE. Its tombs contained urns and grave goods such as daggers and amulets. The 1st-century BCE Tomb of Statilius Taurus was decorated with frescoes depicting the story of Aeneas.

RIGHT AND OVERLEAF:
Vatican Necropolis
Today lying under the Vatican, this necropolis was once an open-air cemetery with tombs dating to Imperial times. A mosaic of sun god Sol Invictus (right) was found in Mausoleum M, while a sarcophagus depicting Christ among the Apostles (overleaf) dates from the late 4th century.

OPPOSITE:
Sarcophagus of the Calydonian Boar Hunt
This 3rd-century CE pagan sarcophagus depicts the Calydonian boar hunt. The boar was hunted by the Greek heroes, as well as one heroine, Atalanta, who provoked a tragic argument by being first to wound it. The man and woman on the lid would have had their faces carved after purchase.

RIGHT:
Statue of Eros Thanatos
In ancient Greece, the god of death, Thanatos, was feared, but for the Romans he became associated with a gentle passing. He was depicted as a beautiful youth, indistinguishable from the god of love, Eros. This statue was carved from Paros marble in the 2nd century CE.

RIGHT:
Statue of Flora
Commissioned by
Hadrian (117–138 CE),
this statue of a young
woman wearing a wreath
of flowers is usually
identified as Flora, the
Roman goddess of spring.

OPPOSITE LEFT:
Statue of Juno
Wearing a robe known as
a chiton, a goddess – often
identified as Juno or Hera
– holds a patera, a bowl
used for pouring a libation
of wine as an offering.

OPPOSITE RIGHT:
Ludovisi Ares
Named for the collector
Ludovico Ludovisi (1595–
1632), this 2nd-century CE
statue of the Roman god
of war, Mars, was based
on a 4th-century BCE
Greek sculpture of
his counterpart, Ares.

PIVS SEXTVS P·M·REST·

Infrastructure

Roman advances in civil engineering allowed the development of a highly sophisticated infrastructure, which was not rivalled for hundreds of years. Many developments were made possible by the invention of Roman concrete (*opus caementicium*), which was used widely from the 1st century BCE and enabled the perfection of architectural forms such as arches, vaults and domes. Rome was one of the first cities with a complex sewer system, the Cloaca Maxima, which may have been constructed as early as 600 BCE. By 226 CE, Rome was supplied with clean water by 11 aqueducts, with a total length of 450km (280 miles). Most of this length was underground, with brief above-ground sections supported by arches. This water supplied public baths, toilets and drinking fountains, as well as wealthy private homes. By Imperial times, Rome was also at the heart of a vast network of well-drained and often stone-paved roads. At the peak of Rome's success, 29 wide highways radiated from the capital. Goods from across the empire arrived along these roads, as well as on barges that were towed up the Tiber from the seaport of Ostia. Goods were stored in immense warehouses, then sold in well-appointed markets and malls. For much of the period, free or cheap grain was distributed straight to the needy. All this infrastructure was built, maintained and regulated by a high-functioning and far-reaching bureaucracy.

OPPOSITE:
Portico Dii Consentes
At the base of the Clivus Capitolinus ('Capitoline Rise'), which led from the Forum to the Capitoline Hill, is the 'Portico of the Harmonious Gods'. This shrine also housed the offices of scribes of the aediles (magistrates).

**Portico Dii Consentes
and Tabularium**

The Portico Dii Consentes
was rebuilt in 367 CE, four
years after Jovian restored
Christianity as the state
religion but chose not to
close pagan temples. The
shrine was dedicated to
the 12 chief deities: Jupiter
and Juno, Neptune and
Minerva, Mars and Venus,
Apollo and Diana,
Vulcan and Vesta,
Mercury and Ceres.

Porticus Aemilia

Built in 193 BCE by the
Aemilia family, the
Porticus was a warehouse
for goods and food. It lay
behind the Emporium
port on the Tiber, where
barges arrived from Ostia.
The tuff and concrete
building covered 25,000
sq m (270,000 sq ft).

Forum of Caesar
In around 54 BCE, Julius Caesar ordered the construction of a public square just to the north of the Forum Romanum. The square was used for Senate business and was surrounded by shops, offices and a Temple of Venus Genetrix, mother of Aeneas and supposed ancestor of the Julian family. Three Corinthian columns (right) of the temple remain.

BOTH PHOTOGRAPHS:
Forum of Augustus
Completed in 2 BCE,
the Forum of Augustus
was commissioned by
Emperor Augustus,
adopted son and heir of
Julius Caesar. Since the
Forum Romanum was
overcrowded, Augustus's
square provided
another space for legal
proceedings, as well as
a location for military
ceremonies. The forum's
focal point was the
Temple of Mars Ultor
('Mars the Avenger').

RIGHT:

San Nicola in Carcere

The 10th-century church of San Nicola in Carcere was constructed from the ruins of the Forum Holitorium and its small Republican-era temples. Six Doric columns of the 3rd-century BCE Temple of Spes can be seen in the church's side wall. Next to the Forum Boarium (see below), the Forum Holitorium was Rome's fruit and vegetable market.

OPPOSITE:

Hercules of the Forum Boarium

This 2nd-century BCE gilded bronze statue of Hercules was found in the Forum Boarium, the cattle market from Republican into Imperial times. The statue was probably in the Forum's Temple of Hercules Victor.

193

LEFT:
Aqua Alexandrina
From 226 CE until the 8th century, this 22-km (14-mile) aqueduct carried water from the Pantano Borghese spring to the 1st-century Baths of Nero. The longest above-ground remains of the aqueduct can be seen in Rome's Centocelle quarter.

RIGHT:
Trajan's Market
Built as part of Trajan's Forum in 100–113 CE, this six-storey, semicircular brick building, set into the Quirinal Hill, housed 150 shops and offices. The edifice was the work of Nabataean architect Apollodorus of Damascus. Additional floors and the Torre delle Milizie ('Tower of the Militia') were added in the Middle Ages.

LEFT:
Porta Maggiore
Built in 52 CE by Emperor Claudius, this gate was erected where the Claudia and Anio Novus aqueducts crossed the Via Labicana and Via Praenestina, the two water channels lying on top of each other. The gate and aqueducts were incorporated into the Aurelian Walls in 271 CE.

ABOVE:
Aqua Anio Vetus
Constructed from 272 BCE, this aqueduct ran over- and underground for more than 40km (25 miles) from the Anio River.

197

RIGHT AND OVERLEAF:
Ponte Sant'Angelo
Known to the ancient
Romans as the Pons
Aelius, 'Bridge of
the Holy Angel' was
constructed in 134 CE by
Emperor Hadrian to cross
the Tiber River from the
city to his mausoleum,
known today as Castel
Sant'Angelo. Three of the
bridge's five arches date
from Roman times, while
the angel statues (overleaf)
were added in the 17th
century.

LEFT:
Ponte Rotto
One arch remains of the 2nd-century BCE Pons Aemilius, known today as Ponte Rotto ('Broken Bridge'). Damaged by repeated floods, it was finally replaced in 1890 by the Ponte Palatino.

ABOVE:
Ponte Fabricio
The oldest Roman bridge still in use in its original form, the Pons Fabricius was built by Lucius Fabricius, superintendent of roads, in 62 BCE. It replaced an earlier wooden bridge.

RIGHT:

Ponte Fabricio
The brick, tuff and travertine bridge spans the Tiber River from the Campus Martius to Tiber Island, location of a 3rd-century BCE temple to Asclepius, Greek god of medicine. Only fragments of the temple can be seen on the island, which is now home to a hospital.

OPPOSITE:
Clivus Scauri
Retaining its ancient name, this road is probably named after Marcus Aemilius Scaurus, consul in 115 BCE. Crossed by medieval arches, the road has maintained its route and is still flanked by the ruins of homes and tabernae from Imperial times.

LEFT:
Porta San Sebastiano
Known to the Romans as the Porta Appia, this gate in the Aurelian city walls crossed the Appian Way. The gate was first built by Emperor Aurelian in 275 CE, then remodelled by Honorius in 401–402. Nearby was an area for parking private transport, since personal vehicles were not allowed within the city.

BOTH PHOTOGRAPHS:

Mamertine Prison
Known in ancient times as the Tullianum, this prison may have been built in 640–616 BCE. Sited near the law courts, the Tullianum was mainly used to hold prisoners for short periods before execution. Legend has it that saints Peter and Paul were imprisoned here. The unluckiest prisoners could be lowered into an oubliette (underground pit). Today, the prison lies beneath the church of San Giuseppe dei Falegnami.

ABOVE:

Porta Asinaria

This entrance was one of eighteen main gates in the Aurelian city walls. Built on the Via Asinaria between 271 and 275 CE, the structure was constructed of concrete and faced with brick.

RIGHT:

Aurelian Walls

By the 3rd century CE, Rome had grown beyond the Servian Walls, built in the 4th century BCE, and was threatened by barbarian tribes such as the Juthungi and Vandals. In 271–275 CE, Emperor Aurelian constructed new walls with a circumference of 19km (12 miles). The walls were 3.5m (11ft) thick, with a watchtower every 100 Roman feet (29.6m (97ft)). The structure was Rome's primary fortification until the late 19th century.

LEFT AND ABOVE:
Appian Way
One of the earliest long-distance roads of the Republic, the Via Appia was constructed from 312 BCE. It was cambered and built from cemented stone blocks over layers of smaller stones. By 264 BCE, it ran to the port of Brundisium in southern Italy. Since laws forbade the construction of funerary monuments within the city walls, many lie along the early miles of the road, including the 30 BCE Tomb of Hilarus Fuscus (above).

OVERLEAF BOTH PHOTOGRAPHS:
Via Sacra
The main street of Rome ran from the Capitoline Hill, through the Forum and – after the Great Fire of 64 CE – past the Temple of Venus and Roma, under the Arch of Titus, to the Colosseum.

BOTH PHOTOGRAPHS:

Ostia Antica

Ostia was Rome's sea port, 25km (15 miles) south-west of the city at the mouth of the Tiber. Today's extensive archaeological site contains structures dating back to the 4th century BCE. Ostia was a thriving city in its own right, with high-status homes, such as the House of Cupid and Psyche (far left), named for a statue found within its walls. The city had a wealth of mosaics, mostly in black and white tesserae of marble, flint and local stones. They depict flowers, geometric patterns, animals, gods and daily life.

OPPOSITE:
**House of Diana,
Ostia Antica**
Extremely well preserved, the House of Diana was a three-storey apartment building, built in the early 2nd century CE. A number of two- to four-roomed apartments shared a toilet and drinking water. The building's modern name comes from a relief of Diana in the courtyard.

LEFT:
**Public Toilets,
Ostia Antica**
The public toilets offered 20 marble seats, each with an additional hole for wielding a stick tipped with a sponge that was used in place of toilet paper. The trough in front of the toilet ran with water for wetting and cleaning the (shared) sponge before use.

BOTH PHOTOGRAPHS:

Theatre, Ostia Antica

Ostia's first theatre was built in the 1st century BCE, but the current remains date from around 196 CE, when the structure was enlarged to hold an audience of 4000. Actors in Greek and Roman plays wore masks to help audiences identify their character type from a distance. The theatre's builders used masks as an architectural motif.

Forum of Corporations Viewed from the Theatre, Ostia Antica
Beside Ostia's theatre was a 2nd-century CE piazza known as the Forum of Corporations. It was surrounded by over 60 shops, offices and guild houses, many with a mosaic that shows what kind of business they housed. There were grain merchants, shipping services and purveyors of exotic animals.

Picture Credits

Picture Credits